HYDRA MEDUSA

OR, GIVE AWAY THE ONE YOU WANT

HYDRA MEDUSA

BRANDON SHIMODA

Nightboat Books
New York

ISBN: 978-1-64362-171-5

Cover art: Manabu Ikeda, "Grass Mantis," 2004
    Pen, acrylic ink on paper
    9 $^1/_{10}$ x 11 $^2/_5$ in.
    Collection of the Chazen Museum of Art, University of Wisconsin
    © Manabu Ikeda, courtesy of Mizuma Art Gallery, Tokyo
Image on page 76: Karen McAlister Shimoda, "Tijuana Taxi," collage, 2021
Cover design by Rissa Hochberger and Kit Schluter
Text design and typesetting by HR Hegnauer
Typeset in Baskerville and Neue Haas Grotesk Display Pro

Cataloging-in-publication data is available from the Library of Congress

Nightboat Books
New York
www.nightboat.org

The desert shimmers at moments as if it owned the whole planet,
and we needed it to be so.

ETEL ADNAN

I had a dream last night that a rainbow was burning.

I had a dream last night that the war fit on the tip of a finger.

I had a dream last night that a scream did not need a hill to gather speed to reach the people.

I had a dream last night that a border wall was built. Carved into the wall were millions of alcoves. In the center of each was a bright red candied apple. The wall was a mausoleum—part altar, part orchard.

I had a dream last night that I met a woman made of bricks. She took herself apart, brick by brick, and became a pile of bricks.

I had a dream last night that my teacher was sitting on the edge of the roof of an old building. She had just given us our final exam, which was to speak extemporaneously for ten minutes on a single subject, any subject. I went last. I closed my eyes, and said: *Someday the earth will become the moon—beaten, abused—extinguished—and yet indispensably radiant to some other life.* Then I stopped. I looked around the room. My classmates were frowning. Then the teacher opened the window.

I had a dream last night that I taught writing to young children on a farm, rolling hills, animals grazing, outbuildings spread acres apart. Day one: I was an hour late because I was trying to make a small book of poems to give to my students, but was not able to achieve more than a disheveled stack of paper. *Sorry I'm late,* I said, *I was trying to make a book for you.* The students were in their seats. I showed them the stack. The paper curled then crackled as if burning. The first book I made, maybe also the last. The classroom was in a small shed with a mossy roof and sawdust on the floor. Ropes hung from a winch mounted on the ceiling. One boy with alert, worried eyes reminded me of a salamander I had seen, years ago, in forsythia.

I had a dream last night that while walking in the woods I came upon a steep hill covered in tree stumps on which children were doing military exercises. One of the children climbed on a stump, pointed at the sun—an eye, with one black spot—and shouted, *five billion years!*

I had a dream last night that I went to a rock opera performed by teenagers. They sang so softly, and the speakers were turned down so low, that nothing could be heard, so the rock opera had to be interpreted by the looks on the teenagers' faces.

I had a dream last night that I was watching a River Phoenix biopic starring a young Yo-Yo Ma (circa early 1980s).

I had a dream last night that I arranged, after dark, in an empty field, four video projectors facing each other in a square. Each projector played a different movie. When I turned them on, the combined throws of their light created a perfect cube composed of all four movies.

I had a dream last night that I was watching a movie that was an eight-hour shot of a young woman pulling long black hair out of the drain of her bathroom sink.

I had a dream last night that I was walking down a narrow street in Beirut. The street was wet, had been hosed down, and was in partial shade. I was not aware of any men, only groups of women. Hanging colors.

I had a dream last night that I hesitated before diving into a pond.

I had a dream last night that I visited a scientist in his home. He opened the door then disappeared. I was left to discover my way through his house. I opened a door onto a dark swimming pool. There were many colorful fish. I dived in, swam below the roots of the house—down through the fish until the fish were all gone. The water above was black, with intermittent vagrancies of dull, trailing light. Below me were rocks, massive rocks. In the crevices were thin threads of coral.

I had a dream last night that I was launched, without parachute, straight into the sky, where I rose above the clouds. At the point where my momentum slowed and it seemed certain I was going to fall back to earth, a ledge appeared. I put my hands on the ledge and pulled myself up. There was, on the ledge, an arrangement of noodles. I was ecstatic: I was not going to starve in the sky! But I also knew that I was not going to return to earth. Noodles were my only consolation. Suddenly, no amount of sky was enough. I was choking. Earth looked, from the ledge, like a fragment of coral broken off a reef. Not only was I not going to return, there would be no reason. Everyone I knew and loved was already dead, by virtue of the fate of endless sky, of having been born, of choking on a coral fragment, and getting used to it.

I had a dream last night that an island folded in half. I called an old woman on the phone. *You know the island you love?* I said. *It folded in half.* The line went silent. I took my glasses off, placed them on a rock, slid into the water. The folded island was covered in small orange flowers. Monkeyflowers. Two utility poles had fallen over. The power lines were inches from the water. *I am going to be electrocuted*, I thought, and the moment I thought it, the sun set. I did not have my glasses, my night vision is terrible, only the power lines and the monkeyflowers were visible. I panicked and started swimming towards the rock where I put my glasses, but I could not find it, because I could not see it. The veins in my body were lightning.

I had a dream last night that I was floating, face up, like a corpse in a coffin (minus the coffin), down a long, low-ceilinged hallway, at the far end of which was a large doorway that opened onto a bright green forest filled with dozens of young, round-headed deer, all of them lying on each other, asleep.

I had a dream last night that death was not called death, it was called *expectoration*. Upon expectoration, a mask—hard, made of something like wood—grows over our face, our face turns to liquid, the liquid cascades down our body.

I had a dream last night that *lispectorate* was a word. A verb meaning *cough up* or *spit out*—phlegm, sarcasm, laughter, disdain—in the manner of Clarice Lispector.

I had a dream last night that a man gave a performance in which he visibly aged. When the performance began, he was young. By the end, he was old. The stage was large. The space for the audience was small, no seats. The man walked to the foot of the stage and said, in a low voice, *My house*.

THE DESERT

As the bus ascended the mountain
and the surveillance apparatus thickened,
I felt the eager learning of children
in my teeth,
and touched my teeth.

Nails had been driven through my teeth
and gums
in four places.

Long nails   long enough
to hold a house together

The mountain was, except for mounted cameras
drones over the high, claustrophobic horizon,
and small black bushes, bare

We were passing through
what westerners believed
was the epicenter of death,

we were headed toward it
returning to it
the west.

the most ritually recursive flame
in paintings of naked figures
turning a massive wheel

that grinds and motivates the earth
to sacrifice its organs
for the wholesale suffering of the people

bearded and asleep,
in the form of bubble-like angels

I pulled the nails out
I could taste the steel.

the occasional insect   shiny object,
clandestine piece of surveillance equipment,
wing of a weaponized mosquito

The landscape was meant to be dreaded,

I could imagine being a child in it, walking with my siblings,
taking a break in the lee of a bush,
thinking about our aunts,
massive pots,
long scarves of ocean

+ + +

A window opens
between trees.

yellow. leaking.   the ocean

has fashioned a cave
into which all oceans disappear.

into caves

that situate dreams
in daring

Families
torn in half, in thirds,
two-thirds, three-fifths,

shed ribbons of tape
in spring,

climb the ocean

+ + +

A shrine burned down
And was replaced
with a shrine

identical   but empty

photographs of the dead
once grimaced from the walls

and the aura of a tree
in the shape of smoke

keeping   keeping

cool
in clay

the dead   a perfect instrument

+ + +

innocence
was emptiness

the calamity of no aura
or shape

returning to its alcove

the dead, Thrown into a milk tunnel,

could only scratch
a simple shrine in a prism

were pitiful
in their performance
A replica of a circumstance

Not even the mountain in the sun
of which the shrine was once

a compliment

seemed alive.

+ + +

A man sat beneath a tree.
The tree was dry, its leaves hammered teeth

the shadows too were dry
and hot

the sun connected
directly

The entire wash
looked like it had served fire
seasons ago.

[The man] sitting between black roots.
was lost, or looking
to lose   what was following him
to the desiccated end of a[n] artery

The man had been walking two days, five days
was stuck
to the ground.

had a toothbrush in his pocket.
hung his teeth on a limb
The toothbrush in its packaging

+ + +

The sun leaked across the hill.

people coming out
of houses   skeletal houses

walk single file

a mountain,   blade.

the next phase
of the infinite,

the mountain cuts through

rain   floods then
footprints of people

+ + +

I approached the altar. colorful
with photographs
of people I did not know.

would never, but now
I had seen them,

as real to me
as people I talk to
but do not see

are alive, loved
deserve to be visited

strangers. go all over the rainbow.

never settle. do not situate
before the gaze of one
particular stranger

The dead were not "gazing"
They wanted it to be over
their reflection to be Stronger,

like a Lunar sound
Materializing
[a hymn of thanksgiving]

to the missing   living?

The living. are late.
always clutching, their face

What a place, faces. immunizations

+ + +

A woman had a clear plastic tube in her left arm
her vein. She needed it
removed.

She pulled it out
a few inches
to show me

it was rooted to her shoulder.

We stood in the doorway of a crowded gymnasium.
No one stopped to acknowledge her.
The crowd's indifference was threatening her stigma,

There were many of her, or one
of many,
with similar needs
that could have been addressed in minutes

but the oversaturation was taken for granted
then where would the women go?

I told the woman I could help her,
let me find someone to help me help her

it was the day after tomorrow,
everyone gathered in the gymnasium
with lighter, more mesh-like clothing

everyone's motion that of people waiting
for a ceremony to begin

a rally
with roses

no landscape   Fireworks

turning   white
embers draining

and the long, drawn sleep
of people who lump their head
against thigh-like bark
for the association of warmth
against 27°
in the desert, January

+ + +

There is, in a kind of clay
the formation of a drum

The clay eats the drum

The drum is not bone
but echoes

the forest   inside a vegetable

Two people have a hard time
relating to people

love
each other

Descend
together   into the river

to pull clay

By drum I mean
machine

through which a thoughtful person might
climb

to reveal the love they found
by hand

+ + +

Three men stood on a hill.
they had been walking three days
two days before that, months before that,

The hill was a short promontory
on which white moons and animals
totems of succor and attraction
inscribed Mirages of these exact men
on every cactus between
the hill and a room with A/C

Are we in Kentucky? they asked.
How many borders do we have to cross

+ + +

land incised by a wall
becomes a beach

on one side only

the people walk

slowly, contemplating
their footsteps

they almost want to repair
what they displaced

almost almost

faces   fake flowers
on the altar

grow maces

+ + +

To show what is the brain, what is beyond

the valley

where a child   spirited up
[an] irresolute cliff

makes the cliff bend
into a bridge

that bind[s] the city,   green
with the skin (the sheen) of

a pistol   flames or

spiders,
for example

pulling apart
anesthetic America:

the stanchion, made of the tendon
of all who have attempted to stretch their bodies across

the current   against the arrows

imprinted with the face
of a mother   doleful, doting

+ + +

The flag is sinew
and flesh   kind of anger

coming
into the lining of
the womb

reconstituting neither fate
nor face

but saints
carved out of whiteness.

The eagle   repulsed
wants to dive off the tip of

the flag, not fly,
but let its small breast

drop
through its feathers

into the dry
riverbed

a gallery of ancestors
expressed the same idea

with their Shadows

+ + +

To sink through the ground of America
is to meet the legions
who have been buried   fall through them

lapse   underground,

commingle, in its original arrangement,   The world

above, the world we think we love is
scar tissue

+ + +

To think of a large country
spoiled
by its intractable people

men mostly   dense as cookies

A country
divided by black rivers

white birds on ice

wings recalling

people on the other side   floating,

careless
somehow eternal

+ + +

The lake was
on fire

Burning pyres

We walked into the wind   the wind was bright lime

steppe fires were suspended
from gallows

Frogs with blinking throats
on top of each other, moving

their arms   to show each other, these are my wigs

And rabbits   a white grasshopper
hopping backwards

water buffaloes   where rapias formed.

a brown braid
hanging from a fence

flower of lice
offered to a cave

devotions, or
two spirits, in

the cell
pushing through

red hot, then

effigies
of someone sleeping, dreaming,

Mourning
is a practical matter

THE DESCENDANT

Cruentation (Latin *cruentare*, to make bloody) is the theory that a corpse will, in the presence of its murderer, bleed. But why would a murderer stick around the corpse he produced? Why would he so handily incriminate himself like that? Cruentation was admissible as evidence in murder trials throughout the Middle Ages. The blood—the bleeding—was the corpse's testimony. But it was more than a reenactment. The blood was fresh. The corpse, bleeding again (it never stopped), was testifying that its relationship with its murderer was not over. The murderer, in being identified by the blood of the corpse, was bound to the corpse for eternity.

In the industry of injustice, murderers are most often acquitted. Eternity becomes a (barely ceremonial) formality. The murderer slips, like a fish, through acquittal. Swims away, becomes trails. To be reconstituted by the weal of impunity. Acquittal is often based on the disproportionate amount of power the murderer possesses, with which they are bestowed, in relation to the murdered. But what if the theory, more specifically the blood, of cruentation could be empowered and extended to measure more than guilt, to express more than indictment? What if the expression of blood from a corpse was the genesis of a curse in which a murderer *inherited the blood* of the corpse they produced? The murderer would become the corpse's descendant, while the dead would become the murderer's ancestor.

These questions come to mind as I contemplate the intransigent, intractable void that hovers a shadow over the ruins of Japanese American incarceration. One element forming the void is the murders of Japanese and Japanese American men inside, outside, and on the perimeters of WWII prisons and concentration camps, murders that exist on and resonate through the continuum of the murder of people of color by state operatives/law enforcement in the United States. The void (shadow) is earth, sky, everywhere in between.

Kanesaburo Oshima was shot and killed by a guard in the prison camp in Fort Sill, Oklahoma. Toshio Kobata and Hirota Isomura were shot and killed by a guard outside the prison camp in Lordsburg, New Mexico. James Ito and Katsuji James Kanegawa were shot and killed by military police in Manzanar. James Hatsuaki Wakasa was shot and killed by a guard in Topaz. Shoichi James Okamoto was shot and killed by a guard at the entrance to Tule Lake. These men are the most commonly cited, if they are cited at all. (An eighth man, Ichiro Shimoda, was also murdered, also in Fort Sill, but the circumstances of his murder are unclear. Shimoda's friends suspected that because he witnessed the murder of Oshima, he was detained by the military police, and died in their custody.) There has been neither justice for nor legitimate reckoning with these deaths. The murderers (both individuals and the systems to which they were reporting) reaped the benefit of passing into oblivion.

What is an ancestor? I have been asking this question, the past few years, of descendants of Japanese American incarceration, many of whom are friends, some of whom are family, some of whom I have never met, but know through their answers. It is an ongoing question. Here, in no particular order, is a very small selection of how they have been answering:

An ancestor can be, in my mind, a familial relation or a non-familial relation (e.g., a political or spiritual or intellectual ancestor). When I think of my ancestors, I think of my grand-

parents and their parents; but, I also see and feel a whole host of living/active ghosts with names I don't know passing in and out of the earth-plane.

I think of all of us as ancestors—just in different phases of the game, so to speak. That is, I don't think of spiritual time as linear, in the way that our time here on earth is. Maybe in some ways it is. But definitely in some ways it isn't. So we're all ancestors... I actually picture a Bon Odori dance when I think of my ancestors — colorful, joyous energy moving fluidly around in an enormous circle... I feel safe knowing we're all connected.

I know that my ancestors travel my bloodline, and that trauma is archived in our DNA. So I feel they are with me and precede me... I believe we're feedback loops.

I tend to imagine them as a chorus of voices that speak to me in tiny hints.

We are a part of their stories, and they are a part of ours. They are the web through time that binds us to the beginning. I like to hope that we are the stalks on branches reaching from them towards the end... I also hope the tragedies and the traumas that they suffered can be healed at least a little bit in me.

Someone who comes before. Someone whose energy I feel passing through me. I live with their wounds, their shame, their proclivities. Their reactions to danger or fearful situations. I've also worked a lot with the concept of the Motherline, and so I feel linked to the women in my ancestral line through childbirth, through pain and sorrow, through the sadness we have all been steeped in since conception—through amniotic fluid, breastmilk, tears. I mother my own daughters with a sense of this weighty, inherited sadness.

Your ancestors are more than just your bloodline. They are the ones who made you possible. Their work, sacrifice, hard-

ships, and joy all resulted in the world you are living in and
the privileges you enjoy. They are not perfect (just as you are
not perfect), but they deserve respect and a place in memory.
You are not culpable for your ancestors' crimes, but you are
responsible for the legacy of those crimes (particularly in terms
of colonialism and genocide) and must strive to do better so that
your descendants will live in a better world.

Ancestors are also benevolent ghosts—who watch over you.

In any case, for me it feels less like something supernatural,
and more like a way of living in narrative.

One book that has accompanied me throughout my thinking, and that is also one of my favorite books, is *About Our Ancestors*, by the folklorist Kunio Yanagita. Yanagita wrote the book in the spring of 1945, as bombs were falling on Japan. He was aiming to articulate the system by which the souls of the dead, which were rapidly being released, would be remembered. It was a question being asked against time. Yanagita defines an ancestor simply as *one who should be venerated*, and ancestor worship as religious communication between the souls of the ancestors and their descendants. His definition appears on the first page of *About Our Ancestors*, which suggests, to me, that definitions are beside the point. That what matters is how an individual *becomes* an ancestor, and, once they become one, how they are treated by the living.

There is the expression or suggestion of a sense, at least, of accountability underlying ancestral presence. Ancestors, having come before—and even, in some conceptions, after—are the conception of both time and space, in other words: *life*, into which we, the descendants, are born, and of which we, the descendants, must take particular care. That is the treatment. Taking care is the first condition of our being born.

Toshio Kobata and Hirota Isomura arrived with 145 other men by train from North Dakota, July 27, 1942. It was midnight. It was a two-mile walk from the station to the prison. Kobata and Isomura were Issei, in their late fifties. Kobata was recovering from tuberculosis, Isomura from a spinal cord injury. They were both walking slowly. Private First Class Clarence Burleson, thinking the men were trying to escape, shot them both at close range with a sawed-off twelve-gauge shotgun. Nine times each. Isomura, a fisherman from Terminal Island, died instantly. Kobata, a farmer from Brawley, died a few hours later. In protest, and in mourning, the 145 men refused to cooperate with the prison authorities. They were put on lockdown. They were eventually removed to the DOJ prison in Santa Fe. The military police gathered up the eighteen shotgun shells as souvenirs. Burleson was charged with murder. The charge was lessened to manslaughter. He was eventually acquitted.

A curse is to fate as pollen is to a flower. It could be said that Burleson was already cursed. That his incorporation into the military apparatus of the United States was a direct consequence, or an essential component, of the curse. That Burleson's ancestors were cursed, or wielded curses, such that their future, their legacy, was fated to be an interminable wilderness soiled and sodden with curses. It could be said, therefore, that the curse predated Burleson's birth, or that his birth was a direct consequence, or an essential component, of the curse.

Burleson's job encompassed a wide range of tasks and behaviors, from staring into the distance while wondering how his parents were doing, to shooting and killing two Japanese men. He might have believed that, in shooting and killing two Japanese men, he was doing his job, because it was not inseparable from it. His job had been created and assigned by a system that was created, in turn, to articulate and maintain the differences between human beings. That was one of the premises of incarceration. Kobata's and Isomura's deaths were predicated on the articulation and maintenance of these differences.

Burleson was a white American man. Kobata and Isomura were Japanese men. They were immigrants, ineligible by law for citizenship. If they had not been murdered, if they had lived ten years longer, they would have become eligible for citizenship. In 1952, Asian immigrants became, for the first time in American history, eligible for citizenship. What would Kobata and Isomura have made of becoming citizens of a country that determined, out of a profuse and historical hatred, that they were enemy aliens? What would Burleson have made of it? Burleson was not any white American man. He was the protector of white American men. Whereas white American men might have fantasized putting a bullet into the body of a Japanese man, Burleson did, and the bullet was government-issue. He arbitrated, in eighteen shots, Kobata's and Isomura's citizenship. He was summoning the law of 1790, which reserved citizenship for *free white persons*. Neither 1790, nor Burleson, could have known that 1952 would come to pass. Nor could Burleson have known that Japanese American incarceration was one of the final tests in the process leading up to 1952. The bullets embodied a conversation he was having with himself. He drew and spilled Kobata's and Isomura's blood because he was afraid of it. He was afraid of it because of what he had been taught. He was taught that Kobata's and Isomura's blood was not only different from his own, but fundamentally opposed. He drew and spilled Kobata's and Isomura's blood because of a grave discomfort, distrust, disgust, even, with the nature of his own blood, by which he was possessed, by which he was being spoken to. White American blood is cult. White American blood is curse.

If a murderer is going to draw and spill the blood of another person, they will have to bear the responsibility of tending to it.

Dear Clarence Burleson,

The human beings you murdered shall become, by virtue of you having murdered them, your ancestors. You shall become their descendant. The blood you produced, the blood that manifested the corpses, shall, between you and your ancestors, be shared. This is more than a contract signed by guilt, more than a relationship formed by grieving, or its disembodied antithesis, haunting. This is blood inheritance. It is a form of account-ability, vigilance and worship, by which your life will hereafter be defined.

As I address Clarence Burleson, or the space, outsized, that he occupies, questions begin to shake loose. If the murderer is cursed with becoming the descendant of the person he murdered, won't that further degrade, by tethering to their murderer, the dead? Doesn't an ancestor have the right to choose the nature and the names of its relations? The curse seems like the formalization of a relationship that already exists, insofar as the conscience of the murderer is not relieved, but inflected, if not wholly populated, forever, by the dead and their death. The dead, meanwhile, inherit, against their will, an association with the murderer that, for being undying, requires an act of severance. (These are the vales/veils out of which ghosts and phantoms—figurations of haunting—stream, continue to stream.) Won't the burden of the curse fall on the dead?

In *Carceral Capitalism,* Jackie Wang reminds us of Mahmoud Darwish's conversation, in his poem "In the Presence of Absence" (translated by Sinan Antoon), between a prisoner and his jailer, in which the prisoner says to the jailer: *You will never be free of me unless my freedom is generous to a fault.* What is a freedom that is *generous to a fault?* A freedom that conjures the power to disburden he who threatens that freedom, who takes it away? Darwish inverts the dynamic, disburdening the prisoner, placing the psychic—the larger, graver—burden of incarceration on the jailer. *He who lives on depriving others of light drowns in the darkness of his own shadow.* Darwish locates freedom in one's conscience, through which he returns the prisoner to the light.

The burden of the curse will not fall on the dead. Ancestors are not burdened, any more than light or memory is burdened. Ancestors, bedecked with colors simultaneously festive and solemn, perform drone-like music on terraces, at the feet of which small children, molded in stone, wearing bibs, listen, eyes closed, to the interlude:

> When the season turns,
> and the colors begin to degrade, the ancestors
> embodying disappearance
> emerge from the grass,
> and form a crest, internal, of music.
>
> a swarm of insects at the bend in the sun
> attack the faithless intruder
>
> and drag him
> down
> through the pore
>
> bleakness   the rhythm of
> transformation
>
> +

The ancestors, bedecked in robes of night
occupy a pantheon

We see ourselves in, imagine
ourselves

in the shapes
of sparest humility,

Hang me in the alcove, I say,
to the future faction
that might draw me out of the well

+

there is, above the crowns of the ancestors
another level of ancestorhood
that cannot be seen

It is the mantle of ancestorhood

insects,   and corpse-like roots
pulse with pregnancy   subliminal enrichment.

+

I dug into the forest   dreamed the sun was a triangle

The bones of watchful guardians
were intact

and warm, and the water
was covered in duck

+

I am returning to my original place
where I would run, get lost,
throw myself on a rock
and turn into the sky.

wind blowing through
eyes threading the vein

But one must go beyond encircling flames. Ancestor worship is a process. The exact nature of the relationship between an ancestor and their descendant is always *to be determined*. The sun on the wall, to the right of the mirror, is hot, and in the shape of a portrait, from which individual personality has been effaced.

I have always conceived of a curse in the negative. That a curse is a punishment, which strips the accursed of their agency. That a curse is a threat to one's sense of self, sovereignty. That if one were the subject or object of a curse, that meant their *self* was being touched, and by being touched, forced into a direction or way of being in opposition to the direction or way of being in which they thought they were moving. This, prior to a consideration of what a curse might be the consequence of, and whether or not it is justified. It did not occur to me that a curse could be positive. That it could be a form of generosity. That being forced in an oppositional direction is exactly what people are desperate for.

It could be said that Toshio Kobata and Hirota Isomura were *cursed*, though it is less easy to say by what. The United States? Japan? The war? Circumstance? Injury? Humanity? Fate? Xenophobia? White supremacy? Racism? Earth? We cannot tap the troposphere to determine the composition of a curse nor to understand how it grows and travels from the mind of one to the soul of another. But that does not diminish, it only exacerbates, the feeling, that in a world—more shortly, a society—that seems intent on evolving in direct opposition to the needs and determinations of those most consistently trammeled and trampled upon, that the only explanation for the ongoing terror, is that a curse has been inflicted, that a curse has been brought down on the world.

There is right now in Tucson a murder trial taking place. The murderer is Lonnie Swartz, a US Border Patrol Agent. The person he murdered is Jose Antonio Elena Rodríguez, a Mexican teenager. Swartz shot Rodríguez sixteen times through the fence separating Nogales, Arizona, from Nogales, Sonora. Rodríguez was in Mexico. Swartz was in the US. October 10, 2012. Swartz claimed that Rodríguez was throwing rocks over the fence and, fearing he might be struck by one of the rocks, shot him. He claimed that, like Clarence Burleson before him, he was doing his job. Regardless of how Swartz's conscience is metabolizing the murder of an unarmed teenager, Swartz, as a representative of the Border Patrol, therefore of the United States, is doing everything he can to justify his actions, in all their brutal extremity. I would not say, however, that he is doing everything he can to relieve himself of accountability. The United States is doing that for him.

As Kunio Yanagita might ask: What will become of the soul of Jose Antonio Elena Rodríguez? What, for that matter, will become of the soul of Lonnie Swartz, who, it could be said, occupies the underside of Rodríguez's death? Will their souls meet? Will their souls have occasion to communicate? Is there science or mathematics inherent within the pairing of their souls at birth, or conception, or in the blind stirring of the immemorial cosmos?

Do homeless ancestors live inside the tree? asks Hoa Nguyen, in her poem "Sacred Ficus Sonnet." Some ancestors are homeless. Some live inside the tree. Some are hungry. Some are homeless and hungry. Some are stretching, expanding. Some are agitated. Some are at peace. The nature of their appetite is mutable, always changing. The relationship between the ancestors and the living is, like a curse, an expression of karmic fluidity. It does not flow in only one direction, but is shared. Ancestorhood is feeding, being fed. Oranges, rice, candy, poems, photographs, incense, a bell whose ring does not travel far, is concentrated, spare, like one's voice in their ear, so that the blood stays healthy, continues to flow. Which should not be confused with being sated. It is constant. I have come to believe something: that life is preparation for the possibility of becoming an ancestor. The possibility materializes through vigilance, responsibility, love. Life only matters insofar as it contributes to this possibility. Have we even begun to get angry?

+ + +

Shortly after this essay was written, a jury found Lonnie Swartz not guilty of the murder of Jose Antonio Elena Rodríguez. Swartz's fear—his perception of being in danger—was given more credence, more space, than Rodríguez's life. The verdict was not surprising. It was crushing. However—and because the fight for

37

justice coincides with the gauntlet of retraumatization—Swartz has not yet been entirely relieved. He will be brought before the public again. A new trial, on manslaughter charges, is set to begin in October.

HOLY WEEK

I wrote a poem about this place
I wrote a poem about a ceremony in this place
I did not know the deer was a brother.
that all the masks were burned

at the end

the people
in masks
were hungry   sleep-deprived

had not slept in forty-nine days

were losing weight   they said
leave your phones
in the car

also: lips

the child comes out   the church

ALL SOULS PROCESSION

A cop almost fell off
his motorcycle.

He was
amid the colorful floral skeletal
commemorations of life,
entertaining the children
waiting for the procession to come down
Bonita

He swerved his vehicle,
almost tipped over.

everywhere   clowns,
evil horse energy

in the pits of their eyes,
dark stele in their hearts,

oversaturating the memorial
antisepsis.

If the cop had fallen
would the children have gotten up?

Who would have been the first
to help?

the police
the perverts of death.

+ + +

The children arrive at night
is one of several meanings of the desert

The children arrive
without knowing

They are
The authorities

measure it
that way

To mimic the disorientation
the mind feels

shocked   to discover the world
has been replaced

with no original   wide
The gate   slides

+ + +

a father describing
in rattled yet procedural terms
the way his daughter flew
across the room
and stuck to the wall

flew across the room
and stuck to the wall,

he said   when he said it,

he was standing
in the center of the room,

pointing to the wall
not looking at the wall,

to be polite?

saw a flower   later
saw the same flower

+ + +

an eight-month-old
face
on the wall,

high, angled down,
like an ancestor   resigned

to her role
as time

and the rooms
in which she grew   and was studied

for a way to be young

+ + +

We stand on the street,
heads hurl through the fork

Man in a truck says Fuck you

all of you—
Disappears—

His range lingers,
but there is river
around

the protest.
is quiet,

where sadness lays

I have trouble calling him *man*
infestation

shoots into the city. cities
that have such sites of contemplation

confrontation

in the dark
daylight.

+ + +

Helicopters at night
describe circles of trauma

belonging to people
hemorrhaging, stuck together

not bringing them
into their future

but outside
the very same gesture

that distinguishes a mutant
from a hybrid

+

when confusion is shared
does it open onto anger
?

helicopters are circling the drain
helicopters are making the drain

perverted in their hunting
perverted in their sweeping the rim

+ + +

Anger turns into a statue

Rainbow
shines

out of People
surrounding   Anger

comes out
voices rise up city hall,

tremble the windows

Down below
Down below

the storm crosses the lawn
people tuned into cascade rebellion

Free the dream. Fertilize.

the call to anger

one person   the spire
the god in each person

Already the answers are light
years behind

people demanding sanctuary
NO MORE RESOLUTION

+ + +

There might have been the aura of salvation in the square
There might have been salvation in the aura of
the square

hole
in the ceiling   cut into the ceiling

or a way to ascend, to mature,

to where the self is renewed   bolstered by
the replication of itself.

shangrila

or less
fortuitous attempts

to rid the world of pestilence

+ + +

A world in which the sources of what passes for life
are reduced to sand

is not a resolution
but a return to the premier state

where a head can fruit
as freely
as be buried

without limit

and with the crispest sun, before the field,

flower   embryonic paranoia.

or the head buries itself

before reaching the more personal end
of punishment.

+

I climbed the steps of the pyramid
to arrive at the small heart

The pyramid was beating.

would it, lifetimes later, bury itself in the sand
force itself to exist
as a dream away from the world

THE GHOSTS OF PEARL HARBOR

Caitie asked me to talk about the mass incarceration of Japanese immigrants and Japanese Americans during WWII, and its relationship to, or its genesis in, surveillance. I should start by striking WWII, since the war, in my opinion, was only the operation of a phase. It begins, for me, with my grandfather. He was born in Hiroshima, immigrated to the United States in 1919. He was classified as an alien, then, after Pearl Harbor, an enemy alien. His name is Midori Shimoda. He exists at the beginning of what and why I write, as I exist at the end of what he endured. I am not here as a poet, but as the grandchild of an enemy alien. In other words, the ghost of my grandfather's struggle to become a citizen, of which my citizenship is the fruition. To be the ghost of my grandfather's struggle is to define citizenship as reincarnation arrested. It is purgatorial. It takes two generations, often fewer, for the government to go from combing lasciviously through your entrails to holding you in complete disregard.

Disregard is not romantic, but administrative. The restitution check my grandfather received from the government was accompanied by a stock apology signed by Bush I. The last sentence read: *You and your family have our best wishes for the future.* The future, fruition, or fruit: *the death of the flower. Endured* is not the right word. My grandfather did not endure so much as he did not die.

Writing about incarceration, reciting its history, runs the risk of letting it pass into the biblical realm, where the suffering of injustice becomes allegorical, therefore instructive, assuaging future suffering with the moral of survival. If the Japanese in America were not embalmed by the psychosis of white anxiety and rage in 1917, 1920, 1932, 1936, 1937, 1940, 1941, then they

51

have been embalmed, in the years since, by the usefulness of their example. The reinvigorated specter of concentration camps—which is, given the inherent structure of the United States, neither exceptional nor shocking—has, in turn, reinvigorated storytelling, by which the lives of human beings, living and dead, are offered up for dissection, towards an understanding of who we are now, which is who we are constantly failing to become.

I am also here as a resident of Tucson. I occasionally substitute at a high school downtown. Recently, one of the ninth-graders told me that embalming fluid smells like cinnamon.

In 1917, the FBI surveilled Japanese plantation workers in Hawaii. In 1920, the FBI surveilled interactions between Asian and Black radicals. In 1920, a plan was created for a Japanese registry in Hawaii. In 1932, the FBI surveilled the entire Nikkei population following the dissolution of US-Japan relations. In 1936, FDR recommended concentration camps to control the Japanese in Hawaii. In 1937, the Office of Naval Intelligence surveilled all Japanese American fishermen. In 1940, the Alien Registration Act required all non-citizens over the age of fourteen to register (be fingerprinted, carry papers at all times), delivering to the United States a comprehensive surveillance database of its non-citizen Japanese.

The surveillance of Japanese immigrants did not begin with Pearl Harbor. Pearl Harbor is a euphemism for the mask of innocence the United States wears to conceal its monstrousness. What seems like the appeasement of white anxiety and rage is their conversion, via fantasy production, into entitlement and pride. Dispossession, forced removal, and mass incarceration was underway well before Pearl Harbor. It was only lacking the kind of *deus ex machina* that would provide its justification.

Deus ex machina: in which an actor, playing a god, is introduced onto a stage by way of a machine. Pearl Harbor is also a euphemism for American fortitude and resilience, which are also masks concealing the retributive face of xenophobia. Xenophobia is a handmaiden of citizenship, and an essential qualification of Americanism. Americanism is not a virtue, but a malignancy. It elucidates a set of cognitive dissonances and defects which produce an animalistic anger that can only find resolution in the treatment of other people as animals.

Every weekday afternoon in Tucson, as many as seventy-five migrants are convicted of reentering the United States without authorization in a mass prosecution called Operation Streamline. The majority of the people are from Central America and have lived, in some cases for many years, in the United States, and are rejoining family, trying to get home. They are sentenced to 30-180 days in prison. There are seven prisons north of here in the town of Florence, Arizona. Thirteen miles southeast of here, on South Wilmot, is Tucson's Federal Correctional Institution. One mile south of that, also on South Wilmot, is the US Penitentiary. One mile south of that, also on South Wilmot, is Arizona State Prison. Five miles southwest of here, on Silverlake, is the Pima County prison. Two miles west of here, on Oracle, is Southwest Key's child migrant detention center. Five miles south of here, on Ajo, is the Pima County Juvenile prison, which was recently being considered for another child migrant detention center. There were, in southern Arizona in the 1940s, seven Japanese American incarceration sites, including two of the largest concentration camps, Poston and Gila River, which occupied the Colorado River Indian Reservation and the Gila River Indian Community, respectively, and a prison labor camp on the mountain just north of Tucson.

Here is a story about something even more local. This story takes place at the University of Arizona: at 12:07 pm on the 3rd Wednesday of every month, a bell is tolled seven times on the University campus. The bell is installed on top of the Student Union, overlooking the main lawn—specifically, the part of the main lawn being occupied by a memorial to the USS Arizona, the battleship that was bombed by the Japanese at Pearl Harbor. It sank to the bottom of the ocean. Actually, it sank *through* the bottom, and landed on the University of Arizona campus. The memorial has converted the main lawn, and by extension the university itself, into the ghost of the sunken battleship. It is comprised of the ship's bridge, containing medallions commemorating the crew members who died, as well as, most ludicrously, a full-scale outline of the ship's deck, imprinted in rubber in the grass. Everyone who steps foot on the grass becomes one of the distinguished dead, or a vessel for their suggestive resurrection. The bell was originally installed on the USS Arizona. Not that anyone within earshot at 12:07 on the 3rd Wednesday of every month would know that. Its alleged use is memorial. Its actual use is nostalgic. Anyone within earshot is incorporated into, and organized by, the bell's nostalgia. Subliminality is not a modification of the truth, but a testament to the ways in which we are being infected by, and made to worship and perform, the national disposition. The bell was tolled on the 1st anniversary of 9/11.

French historian Alain Corbin writes in *Village Bells* about the *prophylactic virtue* of bells, that bells *preserve the space of a community from all conceivable threats.*

Demons were horrified by the sound of bells, he writes. *Bells were credited with the power to cleanse the air of every infernal presence.*

In 1893, the United States, led by thirteen white businessmen and politicians, overthrew Queen Lili'uokalani and the Kingdom of Hawaii. The naval base at Pearl Harbor was established. The memorial on the University of Arizona campus is as much a memorial to the naval base and ship, as it is to the tradition of the invasion and occupation of indigenous land and the land's conversion into an armory. For me it is also an anti-memorial to Japanese American incarceration, and the atomic bombings of Nagasaki and Hiroshima.

One of the early proposals for deploying the bomb on Hiroshima was to release, in the seconds before the bomb, a siren, so loud that everyone on the ground would hear it, look up, and be blinded, a second later, by the flash. By blinded I mean: their eyes would melt.

What could Pearl Harbor and the bell possibly mean in southern Arizona today? Ten miles down the highway from the University of Arizona is a second, 1,345-acre campus, Tech Park, where the University is facilitating the development of the most advanced border-security and border-enforcement technology in the world. It is important to acknowledge institutions that summon old, entrenched atrocities, while actively dreaming and preparing for new ones. The University was awarded a $17 billion grant from the Department of Homeland Security, which they used to create the Center for Excellence on Border Security and Immigration. Todd Miller writes in *Border Patrol Nation* about how students in the Aerospace Mechanical Engineering department have been study-ing the wings of locusts to develop miniature surveillance drones that can fit through cracks in walls. This renders anachronistic the methods used against Japanese immigrants—wiretapping, opening mail, breaking into bank accounts. But anachronisms are the rhetoric of revisionism, which enable, by comparison, the production of more terroristic forms of technology.

The bell, meanwhile, functions through what Simone Browne describes in *Dark Matters* as: *ceremonial terror*. Part of the ceremony is the suggestive resurrection of the dead, whose footfalls form the erotic undertones of, in this case, academia. The stretch of highway that leads to Tech Park is called the Pearl Harbor Memorial Highway. The bell is Tech Park's ancestor, calling—faithfully, angelically—into the future, where it is being answered by technology that is satisfying the bell's dream of a white nationalist paradise—in which anxiety and rage are enshrined in the transmutation of the ashes of women and children on the banks of rivers, of the bones of migrants in the desert, into souvenirs. It is only within the reality of these conditions that a person might be able to stride onto the bridge of the ghost-ship USS Arizona and, infused by the emanations of its panoptic, *prophylactic* bell, feel the entitlement and pride of being an uncontested citizen of what is, in essence, a rapidly and relentlessly expanding graveyard.

OPERATION CROSSROADS

The shape of the explosion
seen from above

answers a question
that eludes

who are living it, unable to see it

the shape
is near

a circle with spurs
a helmet with straps
a jellyfish   bomb

where the shape is deepest
an interior, conjugation of hell

shapes the cyc(s),
from which life forms emerge

is why hell permits
an intimation of itself
in the rift

where darkness is collected
and harnessed

as the voices of people   float on,

let the questions declare themselves
to the echoes

OPERATION CROSSROADS

a face is momentarily suggested
in the old growth environment
of hollow annihilation

an organic form
exudes

itself
over and over

the expectation is remote
the organic form satisfies
the shadows that bind
the heads of survivors

+

It took humans long enough
to invent destruction
in growing old

To discover how organisms grow

old fast
while   destroying

everything
around them

SAN XAVIER

The white cross on the hill of rocks
is a house without light
over the greenest fields in the valley

The virgin, embedded in rocks
prepared the white cross
with the attributes of lightlessness

that illuminate subterranean life

where the cross enters earth
children lay flowers

the cross turns at night
into snakes

+

The wooden effigy of San Xavier
dreams, in his box, of Japan

Houses gleaming with ceramic carnations
fish
sun
mushroom   foam on a river

the smell of salt
broths
socks

grass   butterflies
grazing

old men weaving
shields for the funeral

+

[San Xavier] dreams, in his slumber,
of the panorama   he conceives
to empty what sustains

No one listened

as he tried, and failed
to articulate the word, the one
enfeebling supplication

+

Dirt-colored birds
fly circles around

the cross   painted every so often
as a reminder

salvation is a thick coat
that often stifles
spontaneous expression

+

I visited San Xavier today. He was sleeping,
surrounded by hundreds of people
in the rictus of their oblivion

marvels carved
in dun-colored feathers

fashioned
as arbiters of justice

Religion is not the mold,

but people
who inject themselves
into its sanctuaries

at the openings
mold
begins to foam,
across smaller, more verminous irises

florid spores become, by virtue of being displaced
thick plumes of confectionary smoke
rising off the sacrifice
of collective desperation

the brain cannot stop
reciting constellations

connecting the several incarnations of hell
where angels are arraigned, sent spinning.

+

where the snake enters   flowers
and rosaries
burn

The white cross
the impermeable mercy

WHERE DOES DESIGN COME FROM

Manifesting forms of resistance
required design

The Japanese consulted the desert

The desert, unknown to them,
had opinions.

Was the desert accustomed to
sharing
?

+

The gardens were oases
predicated on the arrangement of stones   stones' opinions.

transfigurations
of time and space

the illusions of time
and space   into effigies

+

Where does design come from. It is teased

requires a period of conscious

and unconscious preparation

in the form of distress:

aspiration   disease.

THE GALLERY

The Japanese gallery was in a European town
the art was in traction

The town was blessed with angelic gargoyles
keeping vigil over moistened streets

Flowers deposed
in every window,

and rivers
pinched
behind every face-like building

I was not allowed to speak
about what I had seen

Even though I could not remember
I was not allowed to remember

to another
who saw it either

standing shoulder to shoulder
staring at a painting of a massacre
from which the sufferers [had] been replaced

to center the camouflage of negative space
that binds suffering to celestiality

what was the seeing after all
but transposing one's latent identity
onto a pattern

to venture its corrosion

+

Japanese artists were relegated to the cliffs
while western artists were permitted to keep their heads

Could open their mouths
as wide as would be
dragging bodies into the furnace

+

The password to get into the Japanese gallery
was Grey
followed by a number   [began with 1]

sympathy for the lightning
defused by the people
with nomadic cerebellums

sympathy for the lightning   the mud beneath the bridge

sympathy for the mud   the erogenous zone
rising formal out of the mud

of all life
art instills
the first sentence

that initiates the drafts
all over again

seascapes? ladders into globe-like
mock orange trees?
wooden puzzles?

THE BOOKSTORE

The bookstore was in the woods.
A creek was filled with leaves.
Reflections were not trustworthy
but still   accurate,
medicinal   Predictive.

The proprietor was Japanese. in his seventies
The bookstore was his house The bookstore did not end
I was in his living room
looking at his family photos.

I was in one.
a baby.
was a glass menagerie. Spies, I thought

I remember one book   stories, set in Shimoda.
The inn was called Shimoda
The baby was not me

Babies live in craters   covered in grass
houses buried up to their second stories
bomb shelters

The man sat at a large drafting table.
What is your name, I asked.
He wrote it in cloud-like letters:
Da. Nagasaki. Nagasakida.
I wrote my name next to his:
Da. Shimo. Shimoda.

The woods
were filled with throats

no clearing   No one read

Books
disintegrating
at the base of trees,

emitting the smoke of spores

to see? Can I live here?

When I get to the end
of the hallway
and enter the cafeteria

I will lose myself
will still be loud to myself
will not be following anybody
will be once again nameless

insignificant
without fingerprints

HIST ODRES DE PARADISE

At the end of the narrow alley
an arch stood alone

what it connected
disappeared

was pure
no parents no profiles
no opposite sides of a valley

or chasm   or stone fantasy

Through the arch
was a temple   yellow money exploding

shadows that mimicked
great grandmother faces

We did not notice at first
the stairs
up the side of the arch   that cut into the arch
where people could sit
and watch the life of the alley

pass into a jar,
sky high with youths eating ice cream

I wanted ice cream too,
to sink into

the arch
the small battlement
the colors on the temple roof
the corresponding fears of old women and men
with that memorial look
which accompanies then defines
the form of ghosthood
that haunts

the possibility of peace
or the imploring of death

the return

THE SKIN OF THE GRAVE

Prepara tu esqueleto para el aire
FEDERICO GARCÍA LORCA

I had a dream last night that a young poet died in Tucson. They were a friend, but we had not seen each other in years. I read their poetry, which, near the end of their life, became prose. I decided to travel to Tucson to pay my respects. I had never been to Tucson, did not know anyone there. I thought I might encounter other poets, some I knew or sort of knew, around the city or at the poet's grave.

Someone told me once that it is irresponsible to visit a museum on an empty stomach. That artwork is sacrificed on the distraction of hunger. I remember thinking, irresponsible? The artist is not a saint, the artwork is not consecratory, the artwork can withstand, is maybe asking for, a little distraction.

Communion. I got hungry on my way to the grave. I asked a woman in the street if she knew a good place to eat. *As far as I know*, she said, *all the lime cuisines are closed*. I had never heard of *lime cuisines*, but they, or it, sounded refreshing. *Lime cuisines* evoked limeade, lime popsicles, ice. Also chilled noodles, cilantro. The way the woman said *all of the lime cuisines are closed* made it sound like the lime cuisines were not only food, but an industry, even a way of life. I asked her what *lime cuisines* were, but she was already walking away.

The graveyard was a small plaza of dirt surrounded by crumbling adobe. The graves were also dirt, some with grass, some of the grass still living, most of it dead. A film about the poet was being projected on one of the walls. It was rough—the wall.

The film cohered on the bricks, but was difficult to see up close. I watched until the film looped back to where I started. In one scene, the poet, shown in slow motion from behind, ran out the front door of a small, dark house into bright sun, then jumped over a narrow canal. From behind, the poet looked like young Federico García Lorca. Their shadow in the canal looked like how I imagined young Lorca's shadow might look: a stingray flying beneath ice.

Lorca was thirty-eight when he was executed by a right-wing militia in the Spanish countryside, near Fuente Grande, between Víznar and Alfacar, in Granada. His body was buried in a ravine. Imagine jumping, many years after dying, over the exact spot where you were buried.

Two businesses were open: a bookstore and a grocery store. The only person in the grocery store was a woman who looked like an aunt I had not seen in several decades. She and my uncle divorced. The woman was walking through the store with four peaches in a cellophane bag. *Excuse me*, I said, *do you know where I can find lime cuisines?* The woman stopped and with a look of great interest on her face said, *Yes*. I relaxed. For the first time since arriving in Tucson, I did not feel that being there was a mistake.

And yet, she did not tell me where. I asked, then, if the peaches were for sale. *Yes*, she said, with the same look of great interest. But then she said, *No, I mean ... These are not peaches, they are apples.* She pulled one of the peaches out of the bag. It was an apple. *Here, take the bruised one*, she said. *The most delicious part of the fruit is the bruise.*

I thought about how the only time I ever saw my aunt unhappy was when, while out on a family bicycle ride by the shore, I ran into the back wheel of her bicycle with the front wheel of my bicycle and she yelled *Brandon, stay back!* I did not notice, until then, that the other apples in the cellophane bag were half-rotten. They looked like small handmade bowls, the texture of dried honeycomb.

The bookstore was the first two rooms of a shotgun apartment. The second room opened onto a small kitchen, and the small kitchen opened onto a room where an old woman was asleep in a chair in front of a small TV. Behind the TV was an enormous bookshelf into which an impossible number of books, mostly small paperbacks, had been mortared. The wall-to-wall carpet was red, brown, and bunched up around the shelves, which were tall and thin, and in the middle of the rooms.

On the second-to-last shelf before the kitchen was a series of small paperbacks, all with white covers, all with the word *SOSTARIA* on the spine, followed by a number, 1 to 100. They were in perfect order, not a number was missing. I pulled out *SOSTARIA 47*. On the back it said: *The 47th volume in the bestselling series of science fiction self-help novels by the world-renowned author and life coach, Sostaria.* I opened to a page near the middle:

"You—you wor————?"

"No."

"I thought of m————ey were resting against the wall, clos————bed. I turned over and reached fo————sli——ped down and made a terrible nois————it——r——e floor. Then I flung the covers o——r m——he——

"What did you want th—ski—ole for?" questioned Freddie, in great ——onde——. "You weren't going skiing."

"I thought I could—cou——st——k the ghost with it," fa————Nan.

————ld————ht—n h——nself no longer, ————a——gh——r, which was in-

————b——————er twin

————TAXI————————ea of

Bo——

"————

"Did yo——————he asked, to hide his confusion.

"No."

"Not at all?" aske————Bobbsey.

"No, Mother. ————er the covers for about a minute—jus————t did—and when I looked, the ghost was g————

When I first visited the graveyard, I was alone, but when I returned, hours later, an hour before sunset, there was a family sitting around a grave. Their presence made me feel that I had not, the first time, been alone, but unaware, because the family looked like they had been there all day.

The film was no longer playing. The wall on which it had been projected was wet. Someone had hosed the film off. The dirt was also wet. Opuntias with bright yellow needles.

Who are you here for? one of the women said. Everyone, except for the children—playing along one of the crumbling walls—looked at me.

Who are you here for? the woman asked again.

A poet, I said. Then, *a friend.*

A poet! one of the men said. *I didn't know poets died!*

They all laughed. Like it was an inside joke.

Poets die first, another one of the women said. She was talking to the man, but also to me, she was looking at me.

They feel things more strongly, don't you think? Although I thought, at first, she said *strangely.*

The grave was a raised mound of earth with clumps of grass. On top of the grave were three cakes. With the family sitting around the cakes, the grave became a table. The cakes were white on paper plates. Blue candles in each, not yet lit.

I knew a poet once, another of the men said. The way he said it conjured images of a love affair, crimes of passion, even murder. Had he really only known one poet? My life was littered with poets—maybe all of my friends were poets—which seemed, suddenly, to reflect very strangely on how I had arranged my life.

I tried to think of the first poet I met, when I was young, too young to know what a poet was or what they did, but in place of an image of a person, was a void of erased air swimming before dark trees outside of a public library. Even then I was reaching, I am reaching now. I cannot remember the first poet I met. Poets appeared, then were everywhere. And yet, maybe it was as true for me as it might have been for the man: maybe I too *knew a poet once*.

Years ago, I lived in Oaxaca. I rented a small house in Xochimilco. The day before I returned to the US, the shower clogged. I removed the drain stop, pulled hair out of the drain, poured chemicals, nothing worked. My landlord, a man in his forties, came over. He brought a snake, a wooden stool, and a glass of ice water. The stool and the ice water suggested it was going to take a while. He put the stool beneath the showerhead, sat down, took a sip of water, then, chewing on a piece of ice, looked up at me, and said, *Would you like to hear a poem? Of course*, I said. *Tell me what you think*, he said, and, feeding the snake into the drain, recited a poem in English—my landlord was Oaxaqueño—about a woman who lived on the top of a mountain, surrounded by—and I remember this exactly—*the ghosts of all the children to whom she wanted to speak but could not*. The children were her children. They all died, all in accidents that had to do with living on top of a mountain—falling off a cliff, getting struck by lightning, entombed in an avalanche. Each child was presented in a description of how they died. The descriptions were brief, a couple lines each. Then the children became ghosts, and the woman returned to grieving. The poem lasted much longer than the time it took my landlord to recite it, if that makes sense. He was moving the snake up and down like churning butter. When he pulled the snake out, it was covered in long black hair, but I was on top of the mountain with the woman, so the long black hair on the snake was the woman, and I felt sad about it.

    My mother, my landlord said. *I wrote it about her.*

He ran his hand down the snake and pulled the long black hair loose. He held it in his fist like he was holding up a head by the hair.

What do you think? he asked.

The hair? Whose was it? My hair was neither long nor black. And why couldn't the woman speak to the ghosts of her children? She seemed, in the end, more ghostly than them, unable, in the poem, to penetrate the membrane that thickened with each one of their deaths. It was as if they were waiting for her to succeed, which is a strange way of regarding the relationship between the dead and the living. I suddenly wanted to put my hand on my landlord—to touch him. I was nervous, and felt—even though, or maybe precisely because, I was feeling it—like I did not know what to say, so I said, *It's beautiful*, and, *did that actually happen?* A pitiful question—I felt sorry for the ghosts—but my landlord treated it kindly.

Two of the women pulled knives out of a cooler. The children, playing along one of the crumbling walls, appeared, for a moment, like candied apples in alcoves. The women started cutting. The grave looked like a body then, breathing.

Who were the women and men and the children there for? Not once had they mentioned a name. Then one of the women looked at me and said, *Do you want a piece of cake?* It was not a question though—she did not say *Do*—but, *You want a piece of cake.*

The young poet and I had been friends, but I realized that because we had not seen each other in many years, there was little to distinguish between our relationship before they died and our relationship now that they were dead. I took for granted, and without much imagination, that the young poet was—like everyone in my life whom I never see—somewhere out there, even though

I rarely made the attempt to put myself there, to be there, to be sure. Now the young poet was dead, and I was beside them. Death is what it took for us to be in each other's company. But what kind of company was I? I felt like a vulture. Sand blew across the skin of the grave.

ANCHOVIES

Kou and I split the anchovies
He never had anchovies before
He did not ask What are they like?

We were like two
in line
for winter

+

If you are prone to happiness, anchovies will not bring you happiness
but like anchovies
climbing up rainbow falls
exist, and will accompany what already exists
in you   if you are prone to unhappiness

only the rainbow falls will remain
charged with the anchovies
lack of endeavor

+

We stood among poisonous flowers,
talked about the foreseeable extinction of Hakodate

The fish are leaving The squid are lonely
Kou's grandparents' house will be sold
new footfalls on the stairs

will be the sound, for a little while,
of grandparents entrenched in their absence

snow will emerge
to tide over the absence,

as challenging death   working with knowing
death's schedule

WORLD PARALLEL

A large yellow fruit
with an aspect of green

is a cold sun   Narrative

Ash gave us a fruit
pomelo, she said

I heard it as: *world parallel*

The sun, having professed its appointments
along the wings of a tree,
had grown cold,
and delicious

+

Sophia invited us over for Pancakes
we gave Sophia   Ash's pomelo

Sophia had a sage plant in the yard.
It was dead.

died, possessed death
as a history

in tribute
to what the sage was not able to

do for
the roots

have eaten everything
lost now
in the ebony magnet

+

Sophia dug and dug
Then sat in a chair

the primal waves of waiting lifted
the need for herbaceousness

as a father's skull
is always adjacent
to a large yellow fruit. a glad smile

beneath the ground
is real

the tomb is light green,
where the dead fruit imagines

a flower   do you know it?

burns my nose

THE SADNESS OF FATHERS

Bodies beneath thin mountainous trees—
shadows beneath thin mountainous trees

are the bodies of men
catching night
at noon

They sleep
on their side

like fish
on ice

beneath narrow skirts
of thin mountainous trees.

+

I invited Kou and Sophia
to the thin mountainous trees

one night,
the snow shook

off The sensation
of separating
from gravity

was as real as
the orbit
and the starlessness of space,

we sat in the grass, where the freefall ends
and talked about fathers
the grimness the sadness of fathers

fathers whirling in empty kitchens,
appealing to a love spun
into a solemn cocooon,

floating there,   yet unable to reach out
and touch

the freshness of nature
as Men in the nightmare

Who were these men?
They walked with their daughters
through the park once

CONTINENTAL PALMS

Masho surrounded by green,   Everywhere
is green   Masho says.
He pats his head   Too hot, he says.

No green to escape   No escape
There is green on top of the mountain, I say
Foolishly

The mountain looks brown   No cloud in the sky
As if to change elevation
is escape

Masho's green is having an outside
sending his sons into the safety
of outside

+

Refugees sitting around a swimming pool
patches of old, fumigated atmosphere
on the bottom

+

I help Masho carry cans, paper, boxes,
heads of lettuce, fruits, chicken
up the stairs, to the table.

Too much chicken. Frozen
heaped on the table.

one table. half the kitchen.
The chicken did not fit in

the freezer
They would have to cook it
right away

to make room.
one couch, one TV,

a bed   pool surrounded by plants

Medicine in the oleander,
for when old men stop speaking,
lose their ability to speak,

and shopping carts riding the walls

+

Green is home, Ethiopia
Masho smiles

He does not want the mountain   the valley
where the cloud
gets caught on a rock

He means where it is cool
where his sons will recognize where they came from
as where they are. Green,

voices
keeping it watered.

FUTURE RUINS

~~Where do you feel safe?~~
Where do youth feel safe?

On the phone
With best friends on the phone

A box
SW Grille

In a car
with sister and mother
eating Eegee's

+

M saw a UFO
K has lupus

A's brother was ill,
the hospital food tasted like her brother's illness

O saw his dead grandmother with lotion on her arms
His father opened the casket
Termites ate the wood

K cried
N cried
when her grandmother died

The last time R saw his mom
they were watching *Family Guy*

L offered to buy him a bike at Walmart

K punched her boyfriend so many times
she blacked out

H, who goes by R, said the healthiest thing she eats is Gatorade

O's grandmother laughed
like a dolphin

+

The teenager from the bilingual school
told me about the skull
that popped out of the dirt
beside her house

She did not say popped,
the dirt was marked

with pores
the grandparents breathed through

the ceiling
the profile of a necklace

fell off
the skull

no salvages in
the quarter life.

+

I can picture you becoming a famous director said Y
who remembered going to a country music concert
with her mom
and how sweaty everyone's arms were

K's father was deported when she was young
They grew apart

Now When he gets home from work
she carries him to bed

+

In the feet
Down the wall

listening to music
behind dark orange shadows

sand
the dry riverbed

The space that exhales

The river
Moving not moving

STIFFNESS OF DEATH

A cow wandered into the desert
was thirsty   tried eating simple white flowers
placed its tongue on a thorn   saw the sun
reel against its white forehead,

A dog leapt over a fence
through the tree
with mint green leaves
over the church   over the man hauling fish in a net

The dog soaked in the sun   was
crushed. in the weeds

Because the dog had blue eyes and was faithful,
tended the loneliness of a man fashioned out of a stump

Because the dog had blue eyes, and was faithful
gifted a man   wounded with the black stumps of earth
with a reason
to skate through the doorway

he died   was found stiff
like a chair
on the side of the highway

The man cried for days, weeks
threatened to grow out of the dog's blue eyes

sprang from a hole
in the darkness   sequestered
along the edges of motion

THE JAVELINA

I saw the javelina from afar
It looked familiar   like a neighbor
eating rocks
at the edge of the grass,   framed by the grass
and several barrels of patriotic flowers

The javelina's front leg was wounded   It hobbled
across the parking lot
to the wash
where it was invited by the shadows
to die   or await the feral weathervane

All mammals grieve, but lack the muscles
to make us feel
the tenderness of the inhuman

Some people let whichever organism is least
apprehensible in its simplicity
hobble
into the splayed gut
fall over   turn into broth

Some people stand where the wounded stood
and grow ornate
with a sense of terrestrial connection
each organism shapes
with its transition

ABUNDANCE

Why don't more animals pass through here? Dale asked
There were none

But sounds
shifting in thick oil
behind the cement wall
that kept precisely those animals out

the moon was rising
a bruise
was rakish
on the moon's right brain

A coyote to the southwest   on the roof of the hotel
birds, nightbirds   a dog

Why didn't more animals pass through
The strangulation of the self
to alert the family   by way of torched skin
and a thin buoy of breathing
to one's individuality
as a service
to extinction   personal in-fruition

+

Is Jupiter red? One star was the question
meeting itself in the atom-sphere

Animals were parading   eating mustards
and ants   fallen fruits

a grapefruit? I asked.
a pear, Dale said.

We were in the sly suburbs, sitting by a swimming pool
The lack of animals was the consequence
of enforcement   the prospectus of looking
at oneself
and seeing an end   the end
when the ark has been sent off
depleted in the mirage of heat
curling the horizon

to the contemplation of the human
on the shore

+

the contemplation is impatient

Why stammer   animals
are on the roof
in the trees   the wall

fences, applications,
hedgerows, motion lights
gates, kitchen windows,

are abundant
Why don't more humans pass through here?

DEATH OF THE FLOWER

There used to be a flower here, I said
Pink and white

the hidden ingredient
passing the storm   pink and white

partners   pachyderms? No.

the flowers did not cool   did not become retrograde,

fell off   blew away?
became dust

+

The flowers have left us, that is their possession,

what remains of us
looking
at where the flowers were

bright   had souls

their souls possessed leaving,
as a station of infidelity   wanton rooms of infidelity

+

the flowers spilled over a wall
stacked tightly with bodies

people hiding against each other
noses pressed into necks,

don't fit like bottles   They drown in
becoming
the wall   pink and white

spilled over, braised,

and decayed
in the gutter,

bitter alloy   so strong and unlucky

were hunted,   run into
the coldest bridges
stargazy

+

There used to be warm meals
sprouting out of the wall,

where the ears are, where bedlam goes

nameless,
people
struggling to perceive their bodies

as if in a movie
set in a graveyard

an air of piracy settles on

+

bodies remember
with their teeth, their toes,   ancient seas
that evaporated before they were made,

on both sides of the wall

miniature suns   ratted hair
limbs protruding below

the field of view
of people rushing home

+

Last night, we saw the river.
We were driving over a bridge,   turned around

to see it
again,   then turned around to see it again.

flowing
towards sunset.

DEATH OF THE FLOWER

I shaved the neighborhood into my arms

the neighborhood grew

wider, more inviting

+

A pomegranate sniffing at our window,
first thing in the morning

withholding, in its womb
a reclining human
made of leaves
and citric implants

is the oversoul
of conception and neglect

does it smell? does it sense what it is
looking for

+

I raise my hand to pull a grapefruit off the neighbor's tree

The neighbors don't tend it
I have never heard water

the oranges max out as dumplings
emissaries of a homesick feeling

not home, not sick
there is no

one home

+

Why do people ask if I like living in the desert?

It is not the desert I like or dislike,
but living

like an angel on fire?

The question (The feeling) remains

ambulant

euphoria, ecstasy
crucifixion

treacheries

and the intimation of water
in the dry dry dirtying.

+

When I think of fruit, I think of friends
Giving fruit to friends   Gestures of goodwill

A friend leaving, going off,
for a long time,
forever.

Here is the fruition.
Here is the death of the flower.

I have not written a single poem this year. From when I woke up on January 1—assuming I woke up on January 1—until today, I have had many dreams, I have gone on many walks, I have, to paraphrase Toni Morrison, willfully created many memories, and I have even written many things, but none of those dreams or walks or memories or things I have written, were transformed—or transformed themselves—into poems. I have, however, read many poems. For example, Mahmoud Darwish's *Mural*, which includes these lines, in Fady Joudah's translation:

One day I will become what I want

One day I will become an idea. No sword will carry it
to the wasteland and no book . . .
like a rain on a mountain that has cracked
from a single sprout
so neither force
nor fugitive justice can win

One day I will become what I want

One day I will become a bird and unsheathe my existence
out of my void. When the two wings burn
I'll near the truth and reincarnate
from ash. I am the dialogue of dreamers. I turned
away from my body and myself to complete
my first journey toward meaning, but meaning
burned me and disappeared. I am absence.
The heavenly and the expelled

One day I will become what I want

One day I will become a poet,
water will be my vision's subject, and my language
a metaphor for metaphor. I'd neither say nor point
to a place. Place is my sin and pretext.
I come from there. My here leaps
from my steps to my imagination . . .
I am who I was and who I will be,
the endless vast space makes me
and destroys me

One day I will become what I want

One day I will become a vineyard,
so let summer press me from now,
let those passing by the sugary chandeliers
of the place drink my wine.
I am the message and the messenger.
The mail and the tiny address

One day I will become what I want

This is your name
a nurse said
and disappeared in her corridor's whiteness:
This is your name, remember it well!
And don't disagree with it over a letter
or concern yourself with tribal banners,
be a friend to your horizontal name,
try it out on the dead and the living, teach it

accurate pronunciation in the company of strangers,
and write it on one of the cave's rocks
and say: My name, you will grow when I grow,
you will carry me when I carry you,
a stranger is another stranger's brother.
We will seize the feminine with a vowel promised to the flutes.
My name, where are we now?
Answer me. What is now, what is tomorrow?
What is time or place,
the old or the new?

One day we will become what we want

Today is September 2. I have felt, since I was a teenager—sixteen, to be exact, a winter's night in New England, to be more exact, on acid, to be even more exact—that life, especially life in the United States, is, at best, the equivalent of the *Garden of Earthly Delights* reproduced on the inside of a kaleidoscope. The kaleidoscope has always been spinning—sometimes slow, sometimes fast. Recently it has been spinning very fast. And I have, also recently, felt myself being drawn further and more irretrievably into its spinning, and into the sanctuaries and seductions of anger and frustration and confusion and depression and delirium and hallucination and jubilation and love that constitute my place in the spinning, and that characterize not only life, but my memory of life, including my memory of what is happening right now and of what has not yet happened. And yet none of these feelings—none of these sanctuaries or seductions—have transformed—or have transformed themselves—into poems. It is only recently that I have been struck by, or slipped into, a realization as to why, maybe one that might even feel resonant. Which is: I am not a poet when I am writing poetry. I am only a poet when I am reading it. Because it is only when I am reading poetry that I feel truly invited into and included within the accomplishment of its thinking, and that I feel animated, made intelligent and at peace. Poetry embodies, for me, an honest accounting of what it means and what it is to continuously test and sharpen and refresh one's consciousness inside and against the collapsing eye at the center of the storm of this atrociously incomprehensible world. Because when I am reading poetry, the kaleidoscope stops spinning; and not only does it stop spinning, it turns inside-out, with every facet of life inflamed, reorganized, and thrown back onto the world; and for a moment, what is atrociously incomprehensible becomes a little less atrocious and a little more comprehensible—and even more rewarding to bear—which, in the motion and the measurement of the kaleidoscope, is so much more than can be expected of this or any lifetime. But, all of that is only a small part of today's invitation.

WE'RE IN THE FLOWER

Look at the orchard, I said.
It's not an orchard anymore, Lisa said.

It's a flower. We're in the flower.

ORANGE LIGHT

I was by the fence. my left foot on a rock.

The lights in Barrio Anita were orange.

I walked on a wide red tongue. filled
with the scent of flowers,
pink lilies.

+

I thought of the monk
with the wide-brimmed straw hat

[Who] made the people absurd
by showing them, without their approval
the right way to pass

+

As the sun went down
behind the sound
the orange light became brighter, then

having adjusted, for every one billion miles,
the sun dropped

I walked until I reached
the deer
I saw legs

10 / 11

It was Lisa's birthday   She turned 143

we celebrated with pretzels
and watched the Descendants of man
fishing [a] manmade lake

The water green   the sky tender,
night trains. strawberries.

wind-stunted skeletons
the outer banks of bad religions.

Lisa had blood in her nose

Fish flew through the air, over the tree,
a woman with a tiny dog   clapping

CATS IN THE DARK

Lisa can see cats in the dark
She saw five cats   I saw four
Because I saw Lisa
stop
and rejoice,

when Lisa turns around
or turns a corner
or keeps walking

cats, twice their shadows
sink down like soufflé

the earth is their egg   the shell rotates

Cats are planets   I cannot see them

We walk one mile   Lisa walks between two
small trees
then walks into a tree   stops
to smell a paper flower.

THE FIELD

two daughters began talking to us,
several more daughters appeared

until there were twelve or eleven

We listened to them explain
The Field—

a place, the daughters said,
we simply had to go.

They gathered at the window
Can we see it from here?

a field with grass and flowers,
No,

How can we explain?
They didn't

try. But you have to
go. Is it far?

a 2 mile walk   Just
follow the road.

We climbed into a makeshift wagon,
strapped Yumi's stroller to the back

the road ended
And we were in the woods

crossing streams
that flowed into waterfalls,

cold   clear
our feet became bare

to endure the moment of pleasure   finality,
because that is where we were
when it ended

the sound of the waterfall
the bold mirror sunk into

the shadow of the pond
to the bottom of the pond
spun into a brown sugar extract

We had been turned loose
had been promised *The Field*,

but virtues were singular, could not be replicated

our crossing the stream
was tantamount
to liberating ourselves from believing, belief

We were deer, a family of deer,
passing into the camouflage mystic

THE HOUR OF THE RAT

We were driving home, west on 17th
past the indoor skate park
when we passed a road we had never seen   a dirt road
with enormous trees arching over

We turned down it
wooden fences, lichen,

A body could filter through
the salvific errands
of kami and aliens

We drove until the road
seemed to end

fields,
and the woods beyond,

density destiny

to the left (the east)
a black boulder formed
a bridge over a creek

The creek soared

Deities posed in the trees
their thoughts   pale and seamless

sent out Starry animations

We stood on the boulder   stared into the creek.
Lisa wore Yumi on her back.
had to bow very low
for Yumi to see the water.

Her first water,   dark and fast
wigs of silver

THE HOUR OF THE RAT

We were in the woods, at first
on a road

in an underpass
feeling safe, 5 pm

We passed a woman and man
setting up their panhandling,

smiling
as if into a mirage

a demon   carnivorous
with a head the size of a planet

the man got scared   ran into the leaves

the woman   wearing fleece
did all the setting up

I wanted to say, No one's coming through
you should go to 4th or

+

The woods
were calm,

we were descending
?
a narrow cliff ledge

mountain goats or mules
might travel

a sheer drop   thousands of feet,

ten miles to the ground
which was, from that height,

earth   the vast unchanging desert

the first generation of skin
shaved down

to the lunar plants

the plaster-white dust
and gray-dust without people

the oasis,   stormed out of itself,

emptied the land
festered f

was a planet
alienating

+

Last night, for example,
we were in a city
the streets were steep
and covered in moss,

we were gliding
down the streets   medieval stones,
cemeteries on every shoulder,

Earlier we were drinking milk with straws
the milk was on the floor   entertainment

We passed an enormous house,
where the mother lived   many boats
stacked on top of each other,

is how a millionaire lives
neverending

with milk

The woman was cagey,
had a child   cauliflower

+

You sing the words of every book,
and the words become soft

you hold the softness in your lap
with a presence in which all earnings are kept,

and emanate
the cologne of policy   occupation

+

Earlier we were on a sheep farm
the sheep were dead,
their bodies denuded, strewn like driftwood

An unseen force was shooting from the sky

was the day before Pearl Harbor
we did not see the sheep being murdered,

as we crashed the woman's house,
slid down the moss
with milk on the floor,
the earth below   empty

+

The cliff ledge was so narrow
I did not think we were going to make it
There was nothing to hold on to

the cliff was white,
the milk had dried,

earth   above the earth
was petrified

milk,
and we were sliding down it.

Remember when we walked freely through the seasons?

Remember?
We live in the desert
Remember?
I have rocks in my hand
We're almost closer
That's tree sap
No, that's a pineapple cleaning
I hear sirens
I wanted a home
I wanted and wanted and wanted a home

Yumi Taguchi, my daughter, two years old (Fall 2020)

NEW YEARS

We stood in the dirt
and stared at the moon

What was the romance between?

It was blood
red and orange, partly

occluded
by the premonition of a planet

that might, one day,
overcome everything
that has been degraded,

to manifest a new birthright

———————————

The moon might lift the house.

all the citruses fatten

bright blemishes teething
in the mirror   fretting

a cold acre
above

the heads of ancestors

They died in a country
of which they were aliens. Enshrined by an alien

evaporating
in the manner of what
will not be remembered

but in burned shadows

+

We fell through the end of the year
to receive our birthright in the desert

We stood in the dirt   We found the sun
in the lush, dead grass.

The moon sank
the occlusion washed over

The moon was the hero deposed
and made to carry correspondence
up the long, arcing ladder

I watched it rise out of the dark tree,
where it was young
and could not yet claim humiliation, then

appear
unadorned

but was bright
with old fire

+

Little by little, the sky eats
The sun and the surface of earth

THE WHITE STRING

One night in late 2016, Lisa and I went to Wat Buddhametta, a Theravada Buddhist temple in Tucson. We lived in Tucson from 2011–2014, left for two years (Marfa TX, Kaohsiung Taiwan, Kure Hiroshima, St. Louis MO, Portland OR), and had just returned. We were exhausted from traveling, and were seeking a place, a structure and a community, in which to meditate. When we entered, the monk, Ajahn Sarayut, was leading a group of fifteen people in a chant of Pali scriptures. He sat on a platform surrounded by tall vases overflowing with flowers—like the severed heads and necks of lithe water birds—and in front of several Buddhas, including, in the middle of all of the Buddhas, a golden Buddha. Looped around the golden Buddha were several white strings (sai sin, in Thai), at least two that were connected to Ajahn Sarayut's wrists, at least one that shot out like spider silk over Ajahn Sarayut's head and onto a wooden grid suspended from the ceiling. The white string passed through the grid, where it seemed to multiply, because many white strings hung down to the floor. The fifteen people sat beneath the grid, each with a piece of white string coiled around their head like frosting on a cinnamon bun. In this way, everyone was connected—to the golden Buddha, to Ajahn Sarayut, to each other.

The chanting intensified and deepened the beauty of the grid of white string, because the rhythmic, cicada-like sound of everyone's voice together transformed the white string from a means of connection into a mycelial form of communication, everyone speaking to each other through the white string.

I am describing all this because I had a dream, last week—two weeks or a few days ago, I am having trouble keeping track—about the grid of white string. I had forgotten about it. But shortly after entering quarantine, the white string returned.

The dream was simple: it was raining. The rain was heavy. And yet there were places, right next to the rain, where it was not raining, as if there were columns of air immune to getting wet. And then, in the middle of the rain and the columns of air without rain, and the sound of it all, appeared Wat Buddhametta, and the grid of white string. Except the room was empty—of people. The golden Buddha was there, white string was looped around the golden Buddha, but Ajahn Sarayut was not there, and neither were the people. The white string was connected to the wooden grid, and many white strings hung to the floor.

The fact that the fifteen people—who, by the force of their chant, had represented the world, or the more infinite world beyond the visible world—had, in my dream, been evacuated from the room, was disconcerting not only to me, but also, it seemed, to the white string. When we attended chanting night at Wat Buddhametta, I paid more attention to the white string than I did to the people, but now, in my dream, with the people evacuated, I missed the people, and felt that something horrible had happened to them, something beyond evacuation, more violent. Their voices? Some part of their voices—some resonance or recollection of pure thinking—existed in the pathetic hesitancy of the white string. And with that, the flash burned out, and it was raining, and not raining, again.

Today is Monday, March 30, 2020. We used to go to the park—five minutes away—so that Yumi could run around. Then we stopped. Now we take walks around the neighborhood. It is spring, trees are green, flowers are in bloom.

to ward off adversity
time speeds up the appearance
of flowers   the children
play

From Etel Adnan's *Time*, translated from the French by the poet
Sarah Riggs.

More flowers, Yumi says, walking through flowers.

A menacing silence has befallen the world. I imagine that the
silence, and its menace, is much louder—even extremely loud—
in places that are not the desert, that are far from, or inversions
of, the desert. As we walk around the neighborhood, people
appear—young people, old people, people on bicycles, people
with dogs—but disappear just as quickly, as if slipped through a
sleeve in the more general mirage of sociality in the age of Covid-
19. Although it feels more like the people *are* the mirage, from
which I cannot discount my family or myself. And it feels like the
world—certainly the wide and languid streets of Tucson—is the
empty room beneath the grid of white string, which still, in our
absence, connects us all, maybe even more intensely.

people come back in our
dreams to bring us their truth
that which our eyes refused
to see, and for which they
burned us, in burning themselves

Etel's *Time* again. I trust my dreams. I trust them especially when
I do not trust myself to responsibly process what is happening out-
side of them. Is that what I am trying to do now, by remembering
my dream, and the night behind it, and the delirious and uncertain

days before it? Because it feels like dreams have perfect timing. What originally appeared as a part of daily life, returns, years later, in a dream, transformed into the legend, or explanation, for life in general. Maybe *explanation* is not the right word. Maybe *legend* is not the right word either. The white string, and the grid through which the white string is disseminated, and from which it hangs down, is powerful because it is precarious. If someone were to pull too hard on any one string, the whole thing might come down. Maybe the grid would come apart, and the white string become so entangled in the pieces, that the entire system might need to be gathered up and carried out into the desert.

Today is Wednesday, April 1, 2020. We just got back from a walk around the neighborhood. There were more—and brighter, more fragrant and effusive, therefore more defiant and mocking—flowers. And, walking through them, were people—young people, old people, people on bicycles, people with dogs—but everyone was keeping their distance. And yet there was—and has been—something beatific about the faces, above the flowers, of people who had spent their day indoors, oscillating between depression and resignation, awareness and forgetting, and the simple agenda of trying to get on.

What is a ghost? A soul that is desperate to return to that which no longer exists? Or the soullessness that has enforced the increasing lack of existence?

We passed a small house with a rusted metal fence. Welded into the vertical slats was a sculpture: six faceless steel figures on a platform. They were like the figures in Giacometti's *Piazza*, but instead of being tall and slender, they were short and squat, as if Giacometti's figures had been hammered, by time and circumstance, deep into themselves. We knew the house, had passed it many times, but had never, until today, noticed the sculpture. *Look!* we said to Yumi, *it's a sculpture!* To which Yumi said, *Sculpture, sculpture, sculpture!* Yumi likes to repeat words, sometimes many times, until she has committed them to memory. Sometimes, when she is excited or tired, she overflows, and a cascade of words streams out of her mind.

Further along, as we walked through a stretch of bright yellow and orange flowers, Yumi bent over to smell them, as she does with all flowers, and declared, simply: *Too many.*

THE BELL

it began to rain
and did not stop

it stopped raining
then started again

the rain slid underneath the skin
that held the desert together

and the people, together

it rained for the span of each lifetime
of everyone who was living here,
or found themselves living here,
or unable to live here
any longer,
but unable to leave

it began to rain   six feet away
from where it was not raining

and did not stop

it smelled like slugs
on the bed   I mean
dogs in the street

the average citizen
did not believe
because they could not see
nor could they feel

distress
and division

through which a perversely sober person might pass
like a sleepwalker through a curtain

+

then a bell rang
all night It rang all night

No one slept But listened
to the bell

framed
by empty urgency

No one could be saved
by a dream

Everyone plunged into
the least suggestive aether

The bell was murmuring   was a seam
torn open

it was windy
The fence flew back and forth

the bell held to the world
by tanzaku, blank,

banging against the skin
of its echoes

The bell stopped   was regrouping

the soul   over the neighborhood
crushed against
the fibers of a nest

bled
bled into the riverbed

flailed
and yet without supplication

slipped out of the skin
It blew against

Who is it
Who is at the gate
Who is at the door

Someone who is hungry
who wants me to be hungry

who brought with them death notifications

Who made it back
I cannot believe I made it back
I cannot believe that I went anywhere and made it back

I should not have made it back.
I feel like I should not have made it back

+

I drank the needle   I put water on for tea
for them. I wait for the water
for them

whose face is it
in the steam?

no water, no steam
no tea
for them

All the leaves are
on the bush

no rest no sleep
I keep them awake

in the middle of the night
is morning for them,

they keep asking
in the form of those closest, with voices

happy new year, is it a question?
is how are you doing? a question

to which I keep answering,

one minute   despair,
the same minute   delirium

I had a dream last night that I was sleeping on the top bunk of a bunk bed. I heard a voice. Etel was on the ladder, touching my foot.

I had a dream last night that I visited Yanara and Robert at their apartment in an indeterminate city. It was raining. I took off my jacket and sat at their desk. Fossils, newspapers in several languages. The ceiling was glass. The rain tapped a beautiful ode. All the lights were off, it was dark, but with wisps of clouded light.

I had a dream last night that Phil and I were walking in a city. It was winter. We were walking down a hill. We climbed down a cliff, over a chain link fence, to a bookstore in an old gymnasium. Rows of cardboard boxes. Phil had a list of books. I had to use the restroom. There was a neon sign above the door that said:

MEN AT NITE
GIRLS + GHOSTS DURING THE DAY.

The toilets were medieval dentist chairs. A tall, slender book by Kenzaburō Ōe.

I had a dream last night that Christine and I were taking a class on haunting (Haunting 101). The classroom was on the second floor of an abandoned building. The first book on the syllabus was Morio Kita's *Ghosts*.

I had a dream last night that it was Jackie's birthday. She showed me one of the gifts she received: a small piece of wire wrapped in green rubber and tied into a butterfly. *It's a filling!* she said, excitedly. Filling like in a pastry or a tooth? Although maybe what she said was, *It's a feeling.*

I had a dream last night that I boarded a long-distance bus traveling very fast through a bright, sizzling landscape. I walked to the back of the bus and there, in the very last seat, surrounded by hundreds of pastel-colored stuffed animals, was Farid.

I had a dream last night that Farid and I were at a dinner party, sitting at a crowded dining table. He turned to me and whispered, *I've been making wooden instruments.* He had one in his lap. Exquisitely precise. He pulled a carving knife out of his shirt and placed it on the table, then handed me the wooden instrument.

I had a dream last night that Youna and I were walking in a seaside town, along grassy rocks hanging over the water, to a graveyard. We climbed over a rock wall to enter.

I had a dream last night that my job was to convince a herd of goats to walk in a circle on the side of a snow-covered mountain. One goat refused: the oldest female. I could see, reflected in her eyes, light from the rising sun shining through dark clouds on a treeless horizon.

I had a dream last night that Lisa and I were visiting a farm. The animals were dead, their bodies across the field. Every few seconds, mud erupted. The farm was being strafed, but the planes, were they drones? were invisible. We ran into a pen, bedded down with the goats.

I had a dream last night that Lisa and I were in the woods, admiring the trees—one horizontal was beautiful—when we noticed that they all had moons hanging from them. An indication of bad weather? Birds abandon their nests and take shelter in the moons? Indestructible. We heard rain, and started climbing the trees.

I had a dream last night that I was in a cult. Cult life consisted of sitting at long cafeteria tables in the ruins of a Japanese American concentration camp and applying lines of whiteout to 8½" x 11" sheets of sandpaper. Straight lines, vertical. I could not get the whiteout to cooperate. My lines were uneven. They wandered and bled. I was given demerits, then handcuffed and escorted to the edge of the camp.

I had a dream last night that I wrote a book about my grandfather. Upset with the book, he attacked me. He had the fortification and the force of all our dead behind him, and they too were upset with the book I had written, so his attack was their attack. I should have given into it, because if their attack was sincere, and if it satisfied the extent of their being upset, then I would soon be joining them, and become part of that force. And yet I tried to escape. I ran into a building. People were eating at long cafeteria tables. My grandfather, catching up to me, started pushing the tables, with the people still sitting at them—he started pushing the tables into me. I laid down on the floor, hoping the tables would pass over. I had, in my hands, with its spine against my neck, the book I had written about him.

I had a dream last night that I took Yumi to visit her great-grandfather's grave. When we got there, his grave was gone, and had been replaced with a white obelisk. Yumi sat down, and, as if knowing exactly how to behave in front of it, closed her eyes. Inscribed on the obelisk were the words: HYDRA MEDUSA.

I had a dream last night that my grandmother, on her deathbed, pulled me close to her face and said, in a faint, half-broken voice, *Give away the one you want.*

ACKNOWLEDGMENTS

Hydra Medusa was written 2017-2020 in Tucson, Arizona, and is the continuation of *The Desert* (The Song Cave, 2018).

The epigraph is from an email Etel Adnan wrote to me on November 14, 2015, which begins, *dear Brandon, we don't know anything you're right, we are chronically misinformed, in fact mistreated by all kinds of official talks which end up being just poison, so we can't think, in the good old basic sense,* and ends, *perhaps that what makes sometimes any stream of water, for example, be so miraculous. The desert shimmers at moments as if it owned the whole planet, and we needed it to be so. Goodnight for tonight x Etel*

"The Descendant" was commissioned by Lawrence-Minh Bùi Davis and Mimi Khúc for *The Asian American Literary Review's* Book of Curses (2018). The responses to the question, "What is an ancestor?" were written by, in the order their responses appear: Brynn Saito, Kimiko Guthrie, Fred Sasaki, Katie Kamio, Elán Rie, Mia Ayumi Malhotra, Elizabeth Fugikawa, Rea Tajiri, and Vince Schleitwiler. They are connected by being descendants of Japanese American incarceration. Thank you to them, for sharing their experience and perspective. Works cited: Kunio Yanagita's *About Our Ancestors: The Japanese Family System*, translated from the Japanese by Fanny Hagin Mayer and Yasuyo Ishiwara; Mahmoud Darwish's "In the Presence of Absence," translated from the Arabic by Sinan Antoon, first encountered in Jackie Wang's *Carceral Capitalism*; and Hoa Nguyen's "Sacred Ficus Sonnet," from *A Thousand Times You Lose Your Treasure*.

"The Ghosts of Pearl Harbor" was presented at "Everywhere It Is Other: Love in Landscapes of Surveillance," a panel/discussion that was part of *Thinking Its Presence: Race, Creative Writing, and Literary Study*, a conference at the University of Arizona Poetry Center, October 21, 2017. The panel was organized by Caitie Moore, and featured Duriel E. Harris, Youna Kwak, Saretta Morgan, and me. "The Ghosts" was later published on *Entropy*, thanks to Janice Lee. Works cited: Alain Corbin's *Village Bells: Sound and Meaning in the 19th-century French Countryside*, Todd Miller's *Border Patrol Nation: Dispatches from the Front Lines of Homeland Security*, and Simone Browne's *Dark Matters: On the Surveillance of Blackness*.

Prepara tu esqueleto para el aire: Federico García Lorca, "Ruina," *Poeta en Nuevo York*.

The image in "The Skin of the Grave" is a collage made by my mother, Karen McAlister Shimoda, in 2021, illustrating a poem that she wrote in 1969. It is included in her "burial" of a *Bobbsey Twins* book from her childhood, in which she "buried" every page behind an original typewritten poem or collage.

[I have not written a single poem this year.] is from the introduction to a reading I organized for *The Brooklyn Rail*'s New Social Environment series, September 2, 2020, which featured six poets I revere: Aditi Machado, Angel Dominguez, Canisia Lubrin, Dao Strom, S*an D. Henry-Smith, and Youna Kwak. The introduction references my relationship with all of their work, and is dedicated to them. Thanks also to Anselm Berrigan, Phong Bui, and Emily Dean. Works cited: Toni Morrison's "Memory, Creation, and Writing" and Mahmoud Darwish's "Mural," from *If I Were Another*, translated from the Arabic by Fady Joudah.

The "The Hour of the Rat" poems are part of a series I handwrote in small, rainbow-colored notebooks between midnight and four during the first months of my daughter's life.

"The White String" was commissioned by Rachel Mannheimer for *The Yale Review*, and was subsequently anthologized in *A World Out of Reach: Dispatches from Life under Lockdown*, edited by Meghan O'Rourke, Yale University Press, 2020.

In addition to the editors mentioned above, thank you to the editors of the following journals and projects where the poems in *Hydra Medusa* first appeared: The Academy of American Poet's *Poem-a-Day* series (Ari Banias and Don Mee Choi), *A Perfect Vacuum* (Judah Rubin), *Berkeley Poetry Review* (Scout Katherine Turkel), *Contra Viento* (Claire Hong and Sean McCoy), *Discover Nikkei* (traci kato-kiriyama), *Gulf Coast* (Devereux Fortuna), *Hyperallergic* (Wendy Xu), *The Iowa Review* (Izzy Casey), *Lantern Review* (Iris A. Law and Mia Ayumi Malhotra), *Neck* (Ryan Johnson), *On the Other Hand: Poets and the Practice of Drawing* (Joshua Edwards), *OOMPH!* (Daniel Beauregard), *The Rumpus* (Carolina Ebeid), *spacecraftprojects* (Gillian Parrish), and *TYPO* (Adam Clay and Matthew Henriksen).

Love to Matt Henriksen.

Much of the writing in *Hydra Medusa* was written and/or revised while riding the Tucson (Sun Tran) bus system to and from work, especially buses 16, 23, 61.

The cover image is "Grass Mantis," a drawing (pen and acrylic ink on paper) by Manabu Ikeda (2004), whose art is also featured on the cover of my book *O Bon* (Litmus Press, 2011). Thank you to Ikeda, and to Makiko Mikawa and Mizuma Art Gallery, Tokyo.

Thank you to everyone at Nightboat Books, Lina Bergamini, Lindsey Boldt, Gia Gonzales, HR Hegnauer, Rissa Hochberger, Stephen Motika, Caelan Ernest Nardone, Kit Schluter, and especially Trisha Low, who saw between the lines and through the shadows of what I was doing and encouraged and helped me to stretch the original daybook across the panorama of its experience.

Thank you to Solmaz Sharif, Dionne Brand, Cristina Rivera Garza, and Wong May, for their words, their works, their support, and their example.

Thank you to the people who appear in *Hydra Medusa*—by name and/or who were with me during the experiences that became the writing—and to the people who accompanied me in my dreams, especially Etel Adnan, Susan Briante, Ash Compton, Phil Cordelli, Dot Devota, Joshua Edwards, Yanara Friedland, Lupita Garcia, Christine Shan Shan Hou, Youna Kwak, Farid Matuk, Caitie Moore, June Shimoda, Midori Shimoda, Dale Smith, Robert Yerachmiel Sniderman, Kou Sugita, Sophia Terazawa, Jackie Wang, Lynn Xu, and Yumi Taguchi Schumaier Shimoda.

Love forever to Lisa and Yumi.

BRANDON SHIMODA is the author of several books of poetry and prose, including *The Grave on the Wall* (City Lights, 2019), which received the PEN Open Book Award, and *The Desert* (The Song Cave, 2018), of which *Hydra Medusa* is the continuation. He is also the curator of the Hiroshima Library, an itinerant reading room/collection of books on the atomic bombings of Hiroshima and Nagasaki, which has had stays in Bellingham, Denver, and Los Angeles.

NIGHTBOAT BOOKS

Nightboat Books, a nonprofit organization, seeks to develop audiences for writers whose work resists convention and transcends boundaries. We publish books rich with poignancy, intelligence, and risk. Please visit nightboat.org to learn about our titles and how you can support our future publications.

The following individuals have supported the publication of this book. We thank them for their generosity and commitment to the mission of Nightboat Books:

Kazim Ali
Anonymous (4)
Abraham Avnisan
Jean C. Ballantyne
The Robert C. Brooks Revocable Trust
Amanda Greenberger
Rachel Lithgow
Anne Marie Macari
Elizabeth Madans
Elizabeth Motika
Thomas Shardlow
Benjamin Taylor
Jerrie Whitfield & Richard Motika

This book is made possible, in part, by grants from the New York City Department of Cultural Affairs in partnership with the City Council, the New York State Council on the Arts Literature Program, and the National Endowment for the Arts.